KT-503-033

THE 'SHAGGY DOG' STORY

by the same author

★

USAGE AND ABUSAGE:
A Guide to Good English
(*Hamish Hamilton*)

FROM SANSKRIT TO BRAZIL:
Essays on Language
(*Hamish Hamilton*)

A DICTIONARY OF SLANG AND
UNCONVENTIONAL ENGLISH
(*Routledge & Kegan Paul*)

A DICTIONARY OF THE UNDERWORLD,
BRITISH AND AMERICAN
(*Routledge & Kegan Paul*)

NAME INTO WORD:

A Discursive Dictionary of Proper Names
become Common Property
(*Secker & Warburg*)

ENGLISH: A COURSE FOR HUMAN BEINGS
(*Macdonald*)

A HISTORY OF BRITISH AND AMERICAN ENGLISH
SINCE 1900
with John W. Clark, University of Minnesota
(*Andrew Dakers*)

Introduction to CHAMBER OF HORRORS
a glossary, by 'Vigilans', of British and American
official jargon
(*Andre Deutsch*)

YOU HAVE A POINT THERE:
A Guide to Punctuation and its Allies
(*Hamish Hamilton*)

THE 'SHAGGY DOG' STORY

Its Origin, Development and Nature
(with a few seemly examples)

by

ERIC PARTRIDGE

Illustrated by
V. H. DRUMMOND

FABER AND FABER LIMITED
24 Russell Square
London

First published in mcmliii
by Faber and Faber Limited
24 Russell Square London W.C.1
Printed in Great Britain
at the Bowering Press Plymouth
All rights reserved

To
CHRISTOPHER MORLEY
who has had so much to do with
the genesis of this lively art-form:
gratefully and affectionately,
ERIC PARTRIDGE

Contents

9

Foreword

So long ago as 1927 I wrote an essay entitled 'The Catch Story'. My interest in this sort of thing has grown with the years. Hence the present monograph.

To the following gentlemen I owe thanks and gratitude for help of one kind or another, generously and promptly given:

Sidney J. Baker, author of *The Australian Language*;

W. M. Beare, Professor of Latin in the University of Bristol;

Edward Clerihew Bentley, inventor of the clerihew and author of *Trent's Last Case*;

Lionel E. Browne, of Newcastle-upon-Tyne;

Raymond Chandler, novelist and short-story writer;

John W. Clark, Professor of English Language in the University of Minnesota;

Julian Franklyn, author of *The Cockney: A Study*;

Foreword

Maurice Goldman, of the Savile Club;

Arthur L. Haydon, formerly Editor of *The Boy's Own Paper* and author of *The Book of Robin Hood*;

Christopher Morley, dramatist, novelist, essayist and poet;

Campbell Nairne, Editor of *Radio Times*;

F. E. L. Priestley, Professor of English Literature in the University of Toronto;

Alvin Redman, cartoonist, author, publisher;

The late Geoffrey Rendall, of the British Museum Library;

Horace Reynolds, American man of letters;

Frank Roberts, of Cotton College;

Angus Scott, artist and cartoonist;

James R. Sutherland, Professor of English Literature, University College, London;

Lowell Thomas the Elder, master of the tall story.

Thanks are also due to the following publishers for permission to reprint or to use matter published by them: Messrs Lippincott and Messrs Faber & Faber (Christopher Morley); Messrs Funk & Wagnalls (Lowell Thomas); and Messrs Hutchinson (A. J. Alan).

I

Origin

The 'shaggy dog' story—occasionally and reprehensibly called 'the spoof story'—has become so popular that by 1952, if not a year or two earlier, it was colloquially known in the shortened form exemplified in 'Have you heard the latest "shaggy dog"?'

As we might have expected, 'the Greeks had a word for it'[1] or at least for its earliest form: παρὰ προσδοκίαν, *para prosdokian*, contrary to expectation: 'used of a kind of joke frequent in Greek Comedy', usually of an unexpected word whimsically substituted for an apparently inevitable word, there being the elaboration τὸ παρὰ προσδοκίαν

[1] This admirable catch-phrase, as I learn from Burton Stevenson's *Dictionary of Proverbs*, was originated by Zoë Akins in her play-title, *The Greeks Had a Word for It*, 929. What dogs they were!

ἐξαπίναιον, the unexpected suddenness or, if you prefer, the sudden unexpectedness. Liddell and Scott quote:

$$ἔχειν\ ὑπὸ\ ποσσὶ—χίμελθα,$$

'to have under [hence, on] one's feet—
chilblains'

where, as they remark, πέδιλα, sandals, was expected.[1]

This sort of trick played upon the listening or the reading public obviously arises from the pleasanter sorts of mischief inherent in all those human beings who take neither others nor

[1] The rhetorical figure occurs also in the Roman writers of comedy.

themselves too seriously, too solemnly, too pompously.

Thence spring both the catch story and the epigram. The earliest story belonging, admittedly rather loosely, to the *genre* is an ancient Greek example:

A pert youth, meeting an old woman driving a herd, called, 'Good morning, mother of asses!' 'Good morning, my son!'

2

Development

It does not fall to me to trace the development of the catch-story, nor yet of that slightly more general type of story with an unexpected ending which may be exemplified by the tale of the two drovers:

During an Australian drought, two drovers stopped one night as usual, to rest themselves and their sheep, or it may have been cattle.[1] After the spartan meal, one man gazed into the remote dusk: 'Horse', he remarked. Joining him, the other

[1] This story belongs to the folk-tale group of the world's stories. I have heard it in New Zealand, Australia, England and Scotland. Naomi Jacobs gives it, suitably adapted, a Yorkshire setting. Wanderers tell these tales, always suitably adapted, the wide world over. In 'A Preamble' to *Tall Stories. The Rise and Triumph of the Great American Whopper*, 1931, Lowell Thomas the Elder makes some very interesting remarks on the subject.

gazed even harder. 'Cow.' Next morning the first man was seen to be packing his few things. 'Going?' asked the second. 'Yes, too much bloody talk around here.'

But not even the most cavalier of casual recounters may omit two extremely significant and pertinent literary examples afforded by two poets of the eighteenth century; the one, an epigram, and the other, a catch-poem.

In 1736 Alexander Pope delivered himself of the following epigram;[1] published two years later:

Engraved on the Collar of a Dog which
I gave to his Royal Highness.

I am his Highness' dog at Kew;
Pray tell me, Sir, whose Dog are you?

In 1760 or thereabouts, Oliver Goldsmith wrote an *Elegy on the Death of a Mad Dog*, published in *The Vicar of Wakefield*, 1766:

Good people all, of every sort,
Give ear unto my song;
And if you find it wondrous short,—
It cannot hold you long.

[1] See Norman Ault, *New Light on Pope*, 1949, p. 342.

Development

In Islington there was a man,
  Of whom the world might say,
That still a godly race he ran,—
  When'er he went to pray.

A kind and gentle heart he had,
  To comfort friends and foes;
The naked every day he clad,—
  When he put on his clothes.

And in that town a dog was found,
  As many dogs there be,
Both mongrel, puppy, whelp, and hound,
  And curs of low degree.

This dog and man at first were friends;
  But when a pique began,
The dog, to gain some private ends,
  Went mad, and bit the man.

Around from all the neighbouring streets
  The wondering neighbours ran,
And swore the dog had lost his wits,
  To bite so good a man.

Development

The wound it seem'd both sore and sad
  To every Christian eye;
And while they swore the dog was mad,
  They swore the man would die.

But soon a wonder came to light,
  That show'd the rogues they lied;
The man recover'd of the bite,
  The dog it was that died.

Goldsmith's poem has passed into folk-tale. Of an old fellow in New Brunswick there is told the story that one day he was attacked by a huge mosquito. He failed to kill, he failed even to ward off, this ferocious creature. When it bit him, tough as he was he let out a yell. But his assailant fared even worse: it died.[1]

The next influence upon the rise of the 'shaggy dog' proper was that of the limerick; this influence has persisted, with stimulation from the limericks and other nonsense-verses of Edward Lear and from the nonsense-verses of 'Lewis Carroll'. The limerick appeared first in the anonymous booklet, *The History of Sixteen Wonderful Old Women*, 1821, an example being:

[1] Based upon a tale in Lowell Thomas's *Tall Stories*.

Development

There was an Old Woman of Norwich,
Who liv'd upon nothing but Porridge,
Parading the Town,
Made a cloak of her Gown;
This thrifty Old Woman of Norwich.

'It was Edward Lear who, by the many limericks in *A Book of Nonsense*, 1846, and *More Nonsense*, 1872, popularized the form.'[1] Perhaps the best of

his imitators was William Cosmo Monkhouse, especially in *Nonsense Rhymes*, published in 1902, a year after his death; attributed to him is the brilliant *Niger* (pronounced *nȳ'gher*):

[1] E.P., 'Nonsense Words of Lear and Carroll' in *Here, There and Everywhere*, 1950.

Development

There was a young lady of Niger[1]
Who smiled as she rode on a tiger;
  They returned from the ride
  With the lady inside,
And the smile on the face of the tiger.

Allied to the limerick, as an influence upon the 'shaggy dog', is the clerihew, devised and perfected by Edward Clerihew Bentley, who in 1905 descended upon a dazzled intelligentsia with *Biography for Beginners*; after a too-long interval, he consented to the publication of *More Biography*, 1929, and then to *Baseless Biography*, 1939; in 1951 the brilliant author of *Trent's Last Case* was fittingly honoured when the publishers of the first book of clerihews issued *Clerihews Complete*.

Two examples will suffice to show the debt of the 'shaggy dog' to the clerihew, that artful-artless verse-form which is so very much more difficult than it looks:

> *What I like about Clive*
> *Is that he is no longer alive.*
> *There is a great deal to be said*
> *For being dead.*

(Boigraphy for Beginners)
[1] Often quoted as *Riga*.

Development

John Stuart Mill,
By a mighty effort of will,
Overcame his natural bonhomie
And wrote Principles of Political Economy.

(Ibidem)

Passing to the medium of prose, I select three catch-stories, not because of merit, which, however, they do possess, but because of their relevance. Current early in the twentieth century was this American story.

Hiram met Lew and Elmer, both laughing their heads off. 'Why, what's so funny?' When at last they could speak, the more coherent of this precious pair said that they had just come from a street fire. Looking up at a frantic figure occupying a twelfth-floor window, they were amazed to see an acquaintance of theirs. 'Hiya, Al. Jump —we have a net, *we*'ll catch you.' Another burst of laughter. 'Never seen anything so funny in all my life.' Becoming impatient, Hiram exclaimed, 'Well, didn't he jump?' This only made the two men laugh still more hilariously. 'Don't you see? There *was* no net.'

'Shaggy dogs' are not callous, but they do owe something to such stories as that and to such dramatic brevities as these two:

Development

Three girls went for a tramp in the wood. The tramp died.[1]

Two men were travelling up to London on a suburban train. Although they were strangers, one looked up from the magazine he was reading. 'Very interesting article here. All about ghosts.'

'Oh, all poppycock, in my opinion. I don't believe in that sort of nonsense.'

'*Don't* you?' said the other—and vanished.

That embryonic ghost-story has been (falsely, I think) attributed to 'A. J. Alan', the famous B.B.C. teller of stories from January, 1924, until shortly before his death in December, 1941.

Rumour has it that he was enlisted by the B.B.C. as a forlorn-hope substitute for someone who had been suddenly and most inconveniently obliged to cancel an engagement. You know the sort of

[1] This story, like so many such stories, tends to reappear in other directions. While writing this momentous monograph I came upon the following:

' "We could have gone over it then when I came in."

' "You were dog-tired," said Martin sympathetically. "I just hadn't the heart. You looked about as fagged out as though you'd gone for a long tramp, and he'd retaliated in kind."

'Ben's face wrinkled up in the ghost of a smile. "I get it," he said complacently, "though most people wouldn't." '

That occurs in a novel published in 1952: *Narrow Shave*, by Stephen Maddock, who himself tells a pretty good story.

situation: hair-tearing; the gleam of hope, 'I know a fellow . . .'; 'Well, let's try him anyway if you *are* sure he tells a good story'; last-minute doubts; 'After all, we'll live it down, I suppose.' His very first broadcast (January 31) took the public's fancy: and when he died, there was, even in those dark days, a general wave of regret, a sighed 'To think that we'll never hear him again!'

There are—or rather were, for they are out of print—only two collections of his stories: *Good Evening, Everyone!*, 1928, and *A. J. Alan's Second Book*, 1932, both published by Messrs. Hutchinson & Co. Ltd. Charles Hilton Brown's anthology, *Best Broadcast Stories* (1944, Faber & Faber) contains three of A. J. Alan's: 'A Coincidence', occurring in *Good Evening, Everyone!*, and certainly one of his best three or four; 'Wottie', from the *Second Book*; and 'The Firebell', broadcast in May, 1937, revived several times and thought by many good judges to be the best of all those told by 'A. J.', as he was affectionately known at Savoy Hill and then at the present Broadcasting House.

'A. J.' was always something of a mystery. Only when he died, untimely, at the age of 58,[1]

[1] In 'Adventure in Jermyn Street', which inaugurates *Good Evening, Everyone!* he mentions that he was born in 1883.

did it become known, to anyone outside a very
narrow circle at Broadcasting House, that he was
a Civil Servant at the Admiralty and that he was
named Leslie Harrison Lambert. And even they
had not known that he was an expert conjurer, a
member of 'The Magic Circle' in its early days and
later a polished, very skilful, original performer
with Maskelyne at St George's Hall; a friendly
witness of his skill has recorded that 'he was very
good-looking and always well groomed—the kind
of man who would shine and excel in any walk
of life.'[1]

I owe most of that information to the *Radio
Times*. The issue of 5 August 1949 printed this
note upon 'Radio's Master Storyteller':

'Nobody who heard him can forget the subtle
voice of A. J. Alan and from time to time listeners
express a wish to hear his stories again. Fortunately a great many of them were recorded. . . .

'Denis Morris, who directs Midland Regional
programmes, is convinced that Alan was the finest
story-teller of radio's first twenty-five years. . . .

'Even now that his identity is known he is still
looked upon as almost a myth. What was the
secret of his hold over his audiences? Perhaps as
near as one can get to defining it is to say that it

[1] From a letter in the *Radio Times* of 26 August 1949.

was a blend of personality, a complete mastery of radio technique, and the ability to invent a thumping good story.'

Leslie Harrison Lambert was no less modest than inventive. In the preface of *Good Evening, Everyone!* he tells us:

'Everything I say over the microphone is taken down in shorthand and transcribed afterwards, and when the idea of publishing my experiences was mooted I began to try to turn them into something like English. However, after a glance at my first efforts in this direction, Messrs Hutchinson's called loudly for the transcript of the shorthand notes, and insisted on using it instead. You must, therefore, blame them and not me if any of the expressions in this book seem to verge upon the colloquial.'

There are some colloquialisms, such as *like* for *as*; the familiar 'you' of direct address; the conversational fluency of the narrative, as in 'Mind you, I *did* think that, once in the car, I should be able to put a few leading questions—but not a bit of it.' Allowing for the exigencies of this very personal, very colloquial storytelling—and who but a crass-head would fail to allow for them?— we must, I think, endorse the verdict that 'A. J. Alan' did truly possess 'the ability to invent a thumping good story'. His stories had variety: they ranged from the merely ludicrous, through the exciting, to the uncanny and, on several occasions, the rather sinisterly macabre. They exhibited much humour, more than a little wit; he could—rarest of gifts—pun gracefully. He was broadminded, yet never lax. He loved and, because he loved, understood humanity. In short, very much a person and a personality, he impressed everyone he met.

In several of his stories, he clearly heralded the 'shaggy dog', as in 'The Tragedy of Hildebrand', which, incidentally, bears a scientific resemblance to Christopher Morley's fable, to be told later. This story was, if I remember rightly, broadcast at some time in the late 1920's. I can tell it but lamely and briefly:

A man had a goldfish, which he regarded with affection and as a companion. One day he took Hildebrand for a stroll in the garden. Both of them enjoyed it. The next day, they went further; the next, still further. By the end of a month, the almost inseparable companions were going for quite long walks, and the leading-strap had been discarded.

For months, all went very well indeed. Hildebrand was now as companionable as the most

companionable dog. They would converse quietly
and knowledgeably, of Nature and human nature.
Then, one very hot day, attracted by the purling
waters of a sylvan stream they decided to cross
it and to rest in the cool of the trees beyond.
Midway, Hildebrand put a fin to his eyes, to
shelter them from the glare reflected by the water:
lost his balance: and fell into the stream.

When Hildebrand's guardian found him, caught
in an eddy only twenty-five yards downstream,
Hildebrand was dead. He had forgotten how to
swim.[1]

Having mutilated Alan's infinitely pathetic story
of that poor little goldfish, I can best make amends
by quoting him at full length and at full stretch.
Read swiftly and gustfully the following tale and
you'll see what I mean:

A Coincidence

This is the story of a coincidence. At any rate,
I call it a coincidence. You may not, however.

The road where I live is very long and very

[1] It is so long since I heard the story that I may even
have named the goldfish incorrectly; 'Hildegarde' would
have been so much more fitting; a friend swears that the
name is 'Hilarion'. Nor has 'The Tragedy' been printed,
so far as I know.

straight. It's paved with wood and well lighted after dark. The result is that cars and taxis going by during the night often go quite fast. I don't blame 'em. They hardly ever wake me unless they stop near the house.

However, about two months ago one did. I mean, he did wake me. He jammed on his brakes for all he was worth just opposite my window, and pulled up dead. You know what a row that makes. Then after quite a short pause he drove on again. That was nothing, of course, and it didn't make much impression on me at the moment. I was only just not asleep. But about two minutes later the same thing happened again.

This time it was a taxi—at least, it sounded like a taxi. Just about the same place the driver shoved on his brakes with a regular scream and *he* stopped. Then I think he backed a few yards, but I don't know. At all events he did a bit of shunting, and in a minute or two *he* cleared off.

As you can imagine, this second business made more of an impression, and when still a third car went through the same programme, I really did try to address my mind to the problem. (I *like* that expression. I once heard Winston Churchill use it.) You know how utterly vague one can be at three o'clock in the morning. I said to myself, 'Oh, yes. I know what it is—it's the same as last February.'

In February, or was it January? Anyway, whenever it was, the water-main bust, and a hole became [*sic*] in the middle of the road. They fenced it off with poles and red lamps, and put a watchman and brazier and sentry-box inside.

That was all right, of course, but during the night a thickish fog came on, and cars came whizzing along, banking on a clear road, and didn't see the lights until they were nearly on top of them, and had to pull up in a hurry. Can't you see the watchman striking out for the shore—after the first two or three?—*mit*[1] brazier.

At all events I thought, 'That's what's happened again. But then I said, 'Hang it all, it's *August*—there can't be a fog—so it isn't that. This must be looked into.' So I got out of bed and hung out of the window.

Presently a large touring car came buzzing along, and just opposite me on went the brakes, and it tried to loop the loop like the others had. I couldn't quite see where it had pulled up because there are trees on each side of my window,

[1] The German *mit*, with. (The Hutchinson version prints it in Roman as though it were an ordinary English word.)

but I heard people get out and there was a general air of excitement for about a minute. Then they climbed in again, the door banged, and away they went.

You can quite imagine how intriguing it all was. I said: 'This cannot be borne for another moment. I simply must go and see what it's all about.' So I put on some slippers and my dressing-gown (pale blue, and much admired about the house) and went downstairs and out into the road.

Beautiful warm night and no end of a moon. I looked up and down but there wasn't a thing in sight, and apparently nothing whatever wrong with the road. So I crossed over to where the marks of skidding began. There were great shining scrawks all over the shop—and then I saw the cause of all the trouble. The moonlight was pretty bright, and about fifteen yards up the road was a patch of deep shadow thrown by a tree. In this shadow there was a man lying. His back was towards me, and his feet were about a yard from the pavement. He seemed to be dressed in light brown clothes—not exactly a check pattern but ruled off in squares, so to speak. You often see girls with cloaks made of that kind of stuff.

Well, of course, I started walking up the road

towards him, but when I got within five or six yards an extraordinary thing happened.

He disappeared.

At least, he didn't exactly disappear, but I suddenly saw what he really was. He was a rough patch in the road—er—don't misjudge me. I'd spent an absolutely blameless evening. No—something had evidently gone wrong with the water-main during the afternoon. They'd come and mended the pipe, but hadn't had time to make good the paving. They'd just shoved the wood blocks back loose, bashed them down with a . . . basher . . . and brushed some sand over the whole thing. Anyway, it produced a perfectly astounding optical illusion. And as if it wasn't realistic enough already, there was a small piece of paper stuck on the road, and it gave a gleam of white just where the collar would be.

Well, I was walking backwards and forwards across the critical point—that is, where the optical illusion ceased to opp, as it were—and you've no idea how startling it was . . . it's a little difficult to describe.

I don't know whether any of you have ever been to a cinema, but the time I went, one of the scenes showed a beautiful maiden sitting on a stone seat by the side of a lake with water-lilies and swans and so on, really very fine, and then, before you could say knife, the whole thing sort of dissolved, and you found yourself in a low-down eating-house in New York, watching a repulsive-looking individual eat spaghetti.

Well, that's what it was like, and while I was coquetting with this effect, round the corner came a policeman, very surprised to see me playing 'here we go gathering nuts in May'—er—so early in the morning. He probably said, 'Here's a gink in a dressing-gown. I'll arrest him—he must be cracked, and I shall get promoted.'

He came up to me with a certain amount of *hesitative*, but I reassured him and said: 'Now you stand just here and look at that man lying there.' And he looked and said: 'Well, I'm—something or other,' and started off up the road—evidently meaning to pick him up. But in three or four yards he got to the place where the mirage melted—and then it really was as good as a play.

He looked—and rubbed his eyes—and looked again. Then he walked to the patch in the road and examined that. And as soon as he'd decided it wasn't my fault, I explained to him how dangerous it was, that all the cars and taxis were shying at it, and one of them might quite easily come to grief. *And* they were waking me up every two minutes. I said: 'If you'll stop about here and warn things, I'll go across and see Sir William Horwood in the morning and get him to make you a sergeant.' And he said: 'I am a sergeant.' So I said: 'Never mind, perhaps he'll make you another.' And I went back to bed.

At about four o'clock there were noises in the road, so I got up and looked out, and there was my sergeant and an inspector doing a sort of fox-trot backwards and forwards—having a great time. No, it wasn't a fox-trot, it was more of a pavan, which has been described as a slow and stately dance, the sort of thing they used to dance in armour. I think they went on playing till it got light.

Well, next day men came and made a proper job of the patch in the road—with concrete and tar and so on—and there it was.

That was in August. Now comes the peculiar part. Exactly a fortnight ago, at about one in the morning, there was the same old noise of a car pulling up in a violent hurry. I was sort of half-asleep, and I said: 'There—the same thing's going to go on happening all night and I shan't get a wink of sleep.'

However, this car didn't drive on as it ought to have done. There were voices and footsteps, and the sound of the car being backed. General excitement. After a few minutes of this I got curious, and again went out—in my blue dressing-gown. The car was pulled up just at the same old place. But there wasn't any optical illusion about it this time. They'd run over a man and he was very dead. They said he'd walked off the pavement right into them.

And now comes the coincidence. He was wearing light brown clothes—not exactly a check pattern, but ruled off into squares, so to speak. You often see girls with cloaks made of that kind of stuff.

Only a person blind and deaf to light and shade, tones and overtones, could fail to perceive the artistry of that story. I didn't hear it myself, but I'm told that it was one of A. J. Alan's ten-or-so most successful broadcasts; its narrative merits are manifest and very considerable. Also: 'A Coincidence' unmistakably represents, on a large scale, very much what a 'shaggy dog' story represents on a smaller. The ending, however, differs from that of the majority of the best 'shaggy dogs' in that it does not constitute a *non sequitur*; it is the perfect dramatic ending. But in its build-up, its 'red herrings', its 'leg-pulls', its circumstantiality and its cosy human touch—in all these, the story resembles a 'shaggy dog'.

But 'A. J. Alan' went much closer than that. He wrote at least one proper 'shaggy dog' story. It lies embedded within 'The Diver', broadcast on Christmas Day, 1925 ('All this and Alan too') and published in *Good Evening, Everyone!* That he should have been invited to deliver so important a broadcast shows how strongly he had entrenched himself in public favour. The scene is laid at the swimming-pool, with adjacent sandwich bar, genially managed by George——, at the narrator's club: a busy scene, 'people darting in and out like a lot of sharks—which reminds me' of a complaint lodged by another member, who, referring to the bar, said:

'I once saw an enormous shark, at least five feet ten inches long, go up to the counter and seize a sausage roll—itself nearly four inches long—and take it away to devour it. When he had bitten off the end, which he did with a single snap of his powerful jaws, he found that it was empty. The sausage, which ought to have been inside, had completely vanished. It had been stolen by another shark, even more voracious and ferocious than himself.

'Never shall I forget the awful spectacle of the

baffled and impotent rage of this fearful monster. He went back to the counter, taking the empty sarcophagus with him, and said: "George, I have been stung!" '

That story was the first genuine and satisfactory 'shaggy dog' to have received the blessing of the B.B.C. and also the first, I believe, to have achieved the dignity of reputable print. These facts, coupled with the tendency of all, or very nearly all, A. J. Alan's complete stories to resemble elaborated 'shaggy dogs', render their author not only a notable pioneer but also the most potent force in the development of the genre. To this, add the never-to-be-forgotten fact that in A. J. Alan we had 'the unexampled story-teller', as Maurice Gorham[1] once called him.

Nevertheless, at least as early as 1905 and current, with a wartime setting, in the Army during the War of 1914–1918, there was a certain story told by those who tell stories, and believed by some (myself included) to be the *spoken* prototype of the 'shaggy dog'.

[1] *Sound and Fury. Twenty-One Years in the B.B.C.*, 1948.

Development

THE MYSTERIOUS NOTE

A young officer, being granted a short leave from the Flanders Front, decided to visit Paris. It was his first visit, and after finding a hotel, having a bath and a meal, he thought he would visit a theatre.

On reaching the theatre his attention was attracted to a large limousine that had stopped at the entrance, and out of which alighted a white-haired old gentleman and a ravishingly beautiful blonde. The young officer, completely bowled over by the fair vision, watched them ascend the marble staircase and, as he watched, noticed the young lady open her small handbag, and in getting out a diminutive handkerchief let fall a small piece of paper. He very gallantly ran up the staircase, picked up the piece of paper, and then hurried into the foyer in an endeavour to catch up to the girl and her escort.

He was, of course, accosted by an attendant, to whom he explained what had occurred, and his wish to personally restore the paper to its owner. The attendant escorted him to the manager's office, and the manager, at once full of sympathy and understanding, took him into the theatre promenade, and allowed him to make a careful search for the young lady, but unfortunately he was unable to see any sign either of her or of the old gentleman.

After this fruitless search they returned to the manager's office, when the manager asked whether the piece of paper was of any importance, and the officer admitted that, whilst it appeared to be a short letter, he was unable to read French at all. The manager then offered to read the contents in order to see whether there was any clue of the lady's identity. The effect on the manager was electrifying, and he immediately handed it back to the officer, rang for an attendant, and ordered him to have the officer thrown out of the theatre at once. This was effected with some considerable violence, in view of his resistance, but he eventually landed on the broad of his back on the pavement.

Being thoroughly incensed at the treatment he had received, he tramped round the centre of Paris for some little while, and then returned to his hotel. The waiter at his hotel expressed surprise at his comparatively early return, and he thereupon unfolded his tale of woe to him. The waiter said that this was most extraordinary, and perhaps he could help: might he see the note? The note was handed over. It produced precisely the same effect upon the waiter, and he at once went away and returned with the manager, who, in handing back the note to the officer, informed him that he could not allow him in any circumstances to remain a moment longer in his hotel, and that he must remove himself and his belongings forthwith. He was quite unable to obtain any explanation of this high-handed treatment, or its cause, and was compelled to pack his bag and leave.

As his anticipated pleasure of his first visit to Paris had been so completely destroyed, he decided that, after all, he would go back home to London and spend the remainder of his leave there.

On reaching London the following day, he telephoned to his fiancée, and was invited by her parents to come out to Haslemere and spend his leave with them. After dinner that evening, sitting with his prospective father-in-law, he explained his original intention regarding the spending of his leave, and all that had occurred to make him change his plans. The father-in-law said that the whole matter appeared to be simply absurd, and he suggested that the young man go up to his room and bring the note down to him, so that his own knowledge of the French language

could perhaps solve the mystery. The young man brought the note down and gave it to his host. To his amazement exactly the same thing occurred, and the note was again handed back to him, and he was requested, not only to leave the house immediately, but also to give his word of honour that, before leaving, he would make no attempt whatever to see his fiancée, and, furthermore, that he would consider the engagement completely at an end and would not again approach her, as he was obviously not the sort of person with whom they wished to have further acquaintance.

He complied and sadly returned to London, feeling that his whole world had turned upside down. While trying to drown his sorrows in an hotel lounge, he suddenly remembered that an old friend of his was a lecturer in French in one of the colleges, and he telephoned him and asked whether he could give him a bed for the night. This request was readily granted and he travelled out to his friend's place. He then unburdened himself of all his troubles since leaving the Line. His friend listened very sympathetically, and, after hearing the whole story in detail, expressed his astonishment, but said that the matter could be very simply resolved, as he had a perfect knowledge of French, and couldn't possibly conceive that any note would cause any similar feelings to arise in him. On learning that the officer had the note with him in his luggage he asked him to go and get it. Some little while elapsed, and then the officer returned, looking very crestfallen indeed; on being asked the reason, he stated that unfortunately he had lost the note.

A prototype, yes; not at all, though at most, points a 'shaggy dog'. It lacks the necessary humour and something of the inconsequence. The *dénouement* is a 'let down' rather than a gaily illogical psychological inconsequence. Compare it with (say) 'The Hole' and you will perceive that it lacks also the warm humanity characteristic of all the longer of the true 'shaggy dogs'—a characteristic for which there is manifestly no room in the short ones. Closer to the ideal is the story of the cake made by a famous *chef* to a special design and then casually eaten in the restaurant by the finicky customer: a story I first heard *circa* 1930. It has been printed in a now rare booklet written by Alvin Redman.

The impetus started by A. J. Alan was increased by three accelerations, all occurring in 1931 and all in the United States of America. But before I deal with these contributory factors, I shall perhaps be permitted to record the fact that I heard my first 'shaggy dog' (apart from A. J. Alan's) in 1929. The story was as follows:

A certain London hostess, addicted to the cultivation of literary lions, invited to one of her sumptuous and slightly eccentric dinners a young Bloomsbury poet with a reputation for very eccentric behaviour. When served with vegetables, he took the cauliflower and rubbed it in his hair. Gazing at him with ecstasy and curiosity, she tremulously asked: 'Oh, do tell me, Mr ——, why, precisely *why*, you do that? Is it part of some marvellously esoteric cult?'

'Do what, madam?'

'Don't be coy, Mr —— I mean, rubbing the cauliflower in your hair, of course!'

'Good heavens!' he exclaimed. 'I thought it was *spinach*.'

Connoisseurs of this sophisticated literary form will recall that that particular story has, at some date since 1945, been adapted. The adaptation runs along these lines:

A regular diner at a London restaurant was one evening interested to see enter a man wearing a stick of celery behind his ear. The same pheno-

menon occurred on six successive evenings. Then
the rugged individualist appeared, with the same
insouciant bonhomie but with a radish.[1] Unable
to contain himself any longer, the regular diner
went across to the oddity and said, 'Excuse me,
sir, but why this momentous departure from the

[1] In another version it is a carrot. In yet another, the
reason is stated thus: 'My wife thinks that the celery didn't
suit my colour-scheme.'

very pleasant custom of wearing a stick of *celery* behind your ear?'

'You are very observant, sir. I hated to break so agreeable a habit. The truth is quite absurd: my grocer has run out of celery.'

To return to the three American accelerations occurring in 1931: the first two, direct and singular; the third, indirect and plural or, rather, collective.

In *John Mistletoe* Christopher Morley relates what he calls 'the fable of the Small Hairy Dog':

'There was a small hairy dog that suffered greatly from heat. So much so that for his comfort his curators often put a small electric fan on the floor. This was highly relished by the small hairy dog, who sat as close to it as possible, turning himself leisurely this way and that to cool. He sat so close to the whirr, however, that when his custodians left the room they always turned off the current, for fear he might damage himself.

'One very warm afternoon they left the dog indoors while they went abroad on some errands. The fan was on the floor as usual, but not running. While they were absent came one of those magically sudden changes of temperature that New

York sometimes enjoys in summer. The wind shifted to the north, heavy torrid air blew away, a cool breeze came rippling in over window-sills, sweeping through the apartment. When they returned, the small hairy dog was sitting alongside the motionless fan, grinning and turning himself to and fro to enjoy the draught.'

That story is clearly in the main line of development towards the 'shaggy dog'; indeed, it has almost arrived. Yet it may have originated as a layman's illustration of the psychological theory —and scientific fact—of conditioned reflexes.

Another American poet, but he as a poet, contributes to the genesis of the 'shaggy dog'. Owing perhaps a little to E. C. Bentley's clerihews and especially to the insouciance of the master's rhymes (compare 'John Stuart Mill'), yet exhibiting always a strikingly original talent and a very pretty wit, Ogden Nash published in 1931 two volumes of verse: *Hard Lines* and *Free Wheeling* (pun on 'free verse'), from which a selection, *Hard Lines and Others*, appeared in England in the following year. I have long suspected that the social satirist that is Ogden Nash has himself invented several of the best 'shaggy dogs' and exported them to England, merely as a token of his amused, tolerant appreciation of the less solemn manifestations of English literature and British humour.

Not quite so close to the goal as Christopher Morley's fable, yet at least as close as Ogden Nash's poems, and clearly set in the main line of development, are a few of the most concise and pointed and witty of the American tall stories current during the twentieth century. Of even the most concise and pertinent, several no less clearly belong to folk-tale; but then, some of the American folk-tales are also tall stories—very tall indeed. In 1931 Lowell Thomas (the elder) published a collection, *Tall Stories. The Rise and Triumph of the Great American Whopper*, which arose from a talk he gave over the radio: listeners sent him tall stories about mosquitoes: over the radio he relayed one of these: others poured in, not necessarily about mosquitoes: he passed a few on to his listeners: others poured in: of these, too, he passed some on to his audience. Hence the book.

The majority of these stories are no more than tall stories. As a result of anxious thought and scrupulously repeated readings, I finally reduced the candidates to five that can fairly be adjudged eligible for the description 'border-liners'. First there is one that bears an odd resemblance to Christopher Morley's fable. For the British reader, this story has to be prefaced with the information[1] that when popcorn pops in large quantities it creates an effect of falling—or of fallen—snow. Of the numerous versions of this widespread story, the following is perhaps the best:

A mule, mischief-bent, wandered into a field of popcorn. In that field there lay an even more mischievous boy, who, seeing the mule, quickly jumped up and fired the dry grass that grew around and among the corn. The blaze soon reached the stalks. The corn began to pop. Despite the heat, the mule, seeing the corn popping and popped all round him, thought it was snow and therefore believed himself to be freezing to death. He died.

Two mosquito stories are worthy of perpetuation.

A boiler-maker in Texas, working inside a boiler, was one day carried off, boiler and all, by a swarm of huge Texan mosquitoes. With their beaks clamped to the metal, they were probably conveying him to the mosquito-ridden jungles of northern South America. A midday factory blew its whistle. Like true Texans, the mosquitoes re-

[1] Such prefatory information, unless very skilfully handled, constitutes a weakness in any story. I have adapted all five stories and retold them in my own words.

fused to work overtime. They settled down, and thus enabled the intrepid boiler-maker to escape.

A farmer kept a cow and a calf out at pasture. If he wanted them for anything—for instance, food—he rang a bell to call them home. One day he heard a loud noise in the farmyard. On hastening outside, he came upon an unusual sight. The mosquitoes had eaten the entire cow, and were ringing the bell to call the calf.

Fish occur in American tall stories even more often than mosquitoes; but then, fishy stories abound all over the world. One particular story is so tall and yet so dramatic that it verges upon the 'shaggy'.

A Florida fisherman, using live minnows for bait, was having precisely no luck at all. In anger and desperation, he dipped a fresh minnow into a bottle of eminently potable and reputedly potent 'moonshine'. Hopefully making a cast, he very soon felt an almighty tug at his line; with a tremendous effort, he managed to haul it in; a huge sea bass was fighting frantically for its life against the minnow, which had it firmly by the throat and was rapidly throttling it to death.

Lowell Thomas's comment is urbane: 'Florida moonshine is liable to make minnows do things like that. It's also liable to make fishermen tell stories like that.'

The fifth story is of a house painter so good at his trade that, commissioned to paint three decoy ducks made of wood, he performed this difficult task with such verisimilitude that a marauding cat, completely deluded, bit the heads off two of them, and the third escaped by flying away.

We have now been enabled to discern the main threads from which the 'shaggy dog' story has been woven: the principal factors operative in the age-long evolution, beginning with 'the sudden unexpectedness' of the Greeks, passing into the epigram and the catch-poem or the catch-story, gathering strength from the limerick, the clerihew and the tall story, and emerging finally as the 'shaggy dog', finest flower of a noble tradition, and acme of the storyteller's art.

3

The 'Shaggy Dog' Itself

The 'shaggy dog' story does indeed represent the acme of the storyteller's art, for it demands a wittily unexpected and sudden ending, all the more unexpected in that the 'lead-in' and the 'lead-up' have had to be deceptively leisurely and almost diffuse; it demands also a considerable skill in narrative, that most difficult of all kinds whatsoever of writing; often it demands, furthermore, an apt and imperceptible mingling of narrative and dialogue. However absurd it may be, a 'shaggy dog' must never be silly.

But example clarifies and enriches precept. It will also serve to indicate the variety and the range.

Example, however, will not explain why and

when the name was bestowed, nor why the majority of 'shaggy dogs' do not concern dogs whether shaggy or smooth. It was not until 1946 that I heard the name applied, although I had known a few such stories since the late 1920's; a creditable friend of mine swears he was using the term as early as 1943. In A.R.K.B.'s 'Editorial' to Alvin Redman's little book, *Somewhat "Shaggy"*, published in 1945, we read an illuminating comment: 'The comparatively recent type of story—the "Shaggy Dog" yarn.' This book contains eleven stories, most of them fully qualified 'shaggy dogs', the two or three exceptions being borderline cases. These stories, by the way, have been fairly popular ever since the middle 1930's: for instance, the monthly magazine *Courier* published a number of them during the period 1937–52. They reached their height in 1951 and maintained it in 1952; nor has there been any falling-off in 1953. 'But why the name *"shaggy dog* story"?' Perhaps for no more recondite reason than that many of the best 'shaggy dogs' do at least concern dogs, some of which are either, like Christopher Morley's early example, 'very hairy', or else downright shaggy.

But the best explanation of the term is that it arose in a story very widely circulated only since

1942 or 1943, although it was apparently invented in the 1930's. The *genre* preceded the name; but then, all *genres* do precede their names.

A householder in Park Lane had the great misfortune to lose a very valuable and rather shaggy dog. He advertised repeatedly in *The Times*, but without luck, and finally he abandoned hope; perhaps also he thought that, there being a war on, it was slightly unpatriotic to make a fuss about the loss of a dog.

In New York an American saw a copy of *The Times* containing the advertisement and he thought that this must be a swell guy, to take all that trouble for a dog. He sought everywhere for a dog that fufilled the requirements, for he was shortly going to England on important business and would have liked to take the replacement with him. At last he did find one. After an infinitude of trouble with a multiplicity of governmental authorities, he contrived to get his own way, for he was truly a very important person.

On the evening of the very day of his arrival in London he telephoned to the Park Lane address and by an unexpected piece of luck was able to talk to the lost-dog's owner, who, heartened by the American's description of the dog he had brought with him across the Atlantic, asked him

to call the next morning. 'I,' he added, 'shall unfortunately not be here. Urgent official business,
you understand. But my very efficient and know-
ledgeable butler will receive you when you call
at half past ten.'

The next morning, at the appointed time, the
American was at the Park Lane door with his
handsome and very, very shaggy dog, which he

had sedulously brushed and combed and over which he had with difficulty restrained himself from shedding a furtive tear. The butler came promptly; but, having glanced at the dog, he firmly shut the door after bowing—and exclaiming, in a horror-stricken voice, 'But not so shaggy as *that*, sir!'

The 'shaggy dog' falls into six main groups: those which deal with dogs, whether shaggy or not; with other quadrupeds; with fish; with insects; with birds; and with human beings—that is, predominantly with human beings, especially with one as the principal character, one might almost say 'the hero'.

A. DOGS

From the fairly numerous British 'shaggy dogs' about dogs, I select five. In only one is the animal said to be hairy, and then merely by implication: the degree of the dog's hairiness does not form a criterion of either the validity or even the credibility of a 'shaggy dog': but since when has credibility had anything—at least, anything fundamental—to do with the matter? As in a fairy tale, suspension of belief is demanded; rather, it is assumed. A certain premiss must be granted—all creatures, including human beings, are, for the purpose of the story, presumed capable of acting in precisely the way, whatever that way may be, in which the narrator causes them to act. To say 'I just don't believe it' invites one of two replies: 'I'm sorry for you', if one feels good-humoured and is urbane; 'Nobody has asked you to *believe* it', if one feels the opposite. To say, 'But it's quite too absurd' is to evoke the rejoinder, 'Of course it's absurd. This story came neither from a Blue Book, nor yet from a White Paper.' To say, 'But surely this sort of thing, although it may be all very well for Sixth Formers and undergraduates, is hardly worthy to enliven the leisure, much less to engage the serious attention, of serious adults?' —that, dear Lady Pomposity, is to take far too grave a view both of yourself and of others. Life to-day is no joke: therefore let us make it one.

Of the five British dog stories, the first exemplifies the entire genre:

A businessman, travelling by train to London from one of its more distant dormitories, so hurriedly got into a compartment that he did not at first notice the other two occupants. Looking up from the financial page of *The Times* he saw another businessman, engaged in playing chess with a magnificent Newfoundland. Being a chess player himself, he disbelieved what he saw, rubbed out of his eyes the residue of sleep and vigorously shook his head in order to clear it. The dog was still there, and playing in an old-fashioned way, reminiscent of Capablanca rather than of Botvinnik.

The players had rules of their own: the time allowed for each move was one minute, but often they needed only a few seconds. Two minutes before the train pulled in at the platform, the game ended, with the Newfoundland a worthy winner.

Unable to restrain his curiosity any longer, the fascinated onlooker said to the other man, 'That's a wonderful dog you have there. He beat you, didn't he? Yet you, sir, if I may say so, were playing very well. Does your dog compete in tournaments?'

'Dear me, no! He's not as good as all that. I beat Newfie in the two previous games.'

An enlightening variation on that theme occurs in this tale:

A man went away for the week-end. He arrived rather late, after dinner. The other members of the house party were all sitting around in the drawing-room and at one end of the room a game of poker was in progress. One of the players was a dog.

After he had been introduced all round, the man said to his host: 'What a wonderful dog. He must be very intelligent to be able to play poker.'

'Well, he's not a very good player really,' replied the host. 'Because whenever he gets a good hand he wags his tail.'

More objective is a story that, appearing in an American newspaper, is yet entirely English. It concerns two men and a dog. The men are taking the dog for a walk along a quiet beach. The owner, thinking to divert his friend and his dog, threw a stick into the sea. The dog walked on the surface of the water and scurried back with the stick. Both men rubbed their eyes and attributed the 'optical illusion' to a rather heavy night. Again the stick was thrown. Again the dog walked upon the surface of the compliant waters. The friend, turning commiseratingly to the owner, exclaimed, 'I'm truly sorry, Bill. The animal simply cannot *swim*.'

A very brilliant dog illuminates the following story:

At a 'local' in one of the London suburbs—so far as that goes, it might equally well have been a Paris or a New York suburb—a regular, of twenty years' moderate drinking, entered a new phase of enjoyment when a stranger began to frequent the bar. Not that he was interested in the stranger; but in the dog that always accompanied him and did so much to enliven the evening.

The first time the stranger and his dog came into the room, which, in an older tradition fast dying out, possessed a rather good piano, the man ordered a pint o' bitter, sat down on a stool, patted the dog's head, and quietly urged him to 'play something for us, Smoky. Something lively.

This dump's like a morgue, we must do something about it.'

To the amazement of the regulars and the pre-paring-to-be-resentful barman, the dog sedately walked to the piano and adjusted the stool. With-out looking round for preliminary applause, nor in fact receiving any, it started to play a very

catchy thing from the most popular musical comedy of the moment. The animal played very well, without any irritating mannerisms or large, pretentious gestures. On being asked to 'play us another, do!' and seeing that this was not mere politeness but genuine appreciation, the modest executant played two other numbers from the same 'musical'.

For many evenings this sort of thing continued. The regulars would ask, now for 'Nelly Dean' or some other sentimental ballad, now for a specifically Cockney song, such as 'My Old Dutch', and occasionally for a more classical piece. One night, while everyone was listening raptly to a most artistic rendering of Handel's 'Largo', a famous music-hall manager strolled in, to quench a raging thirst. Suddenly the visitor realized that, whoever was playing, he certainly 'knew his stuff'. He was amazed to see that it was a dog, a very ordinary-looking dog. 'Surely not,' he muttered to himself, 'it's far too early for that.'

'Plays well, don't you think?' remarked the dog's owner.

'He sure does. Would he play "The Warsaw Concerto"?'

'Piece of cake. Hey there, play "The Warsaw"

for the gentleman, will you? And don't pull your punches.'

The dog played this spectacular piece with spectacular virtuosity.

'Anything else you'd like?'

'Yes, Liszt's "Hungarian Rhapsody"—that very fast, difficult one all the most florid pianists love to play—and so seldom can.' (That'll fox him, he thought; this bloke won't know the meaning of 'florid' . . . not at all sure I do myself; anyway, the dog'll never have heard of Liszt, but if I'm wrong, it'll prove that the creature's good, so good that I'll sign it up.)

The 'canine pianist'—already the astute music-hall manager was composing an advertisement—had no trouble in dealing with this example of musical pyrotechnics. Bewildered, the manager, not because he wished to know but simply because he hated to give himself away to these simpletons of the suburbs, blurted:

'Yes, the dog is good; in fact, marvellous.' Pause. 'By the way, can the animal orchestrate?'

'Orchestrate? Don't be silly! Haven't you noticed that my dog is a bitch?'[1]

[1] That, more or less, is how the story is usually told; that, exactly, is the wording of the owner's final speech. By the majority, the story is thought to stand very

That bitch may or may not have been shaggy. The two dogs in the next story were perhaps shaggy; it doesn't in the least matter whether they were or not. Like the preceding tale, this one also takes place in a public-house, as so many of the best 'shaggy dogs' tend to do, perhaps because the 'public' is the ordinary man's club. (I don't know a single good 'shaggy dog' with a club setting; yet, like the public-house and the Stock Exchange, the club is one of the most fertile nurseries of this type of story.)

A man had two dogs. He was very fond of them and took them with him whenever he went to his 'local' in the evening. Well-behaved, they did him credit and never caused him the slightest embarrassment; as he would sometimes admit, he was rather proud of them.

At the 'pub' he would seat himself always on the same stool. On his right, Fido would sit; on his left, Lassie. He would order a mild-and-bitter for himself and a small gin for each of the dogs. Although he never dawdled, the man would drink in a leisurely way. The two dogs genteelly sipped

satisfactorily on its external merits. It does. By the Greek scholar and by the etymologist, however, the conclusion is enjoyed for another reason.

their gins and usually finished level with their master: and over their masks a beatific grin would slowly creep, without, however, the slightest loss of decorum. As soon as they had finished their drinks—they never took more than one—they went out quietly and quietly walked home in perfect companionship.

The barman soon came to recognize them as regular and orderly customers and perhaps to regard them as an asset, so that when, one evening, the two dogs arrived without their master and hopped up on to their customary stools, he served them with the customary gin apiece and, when Fido gallantly offered to pay, waved the offer aside with an easy and courteous gesture.

The next night, the two dogs returned, their master with them, and sat down as usual. To the barman, their master said, 'I owe you for two gins. Take the price out of this note. And, by the way, I'd like to thank you for being so good to these two. They've got so used to their nightly tot that they miss it—miss it very much, I fear. To show you that they and I appreciate your kindness, I want you to accept this small lobster.'

'Thank you very much, sir. I'll take it home for supper.'

'Oh no, don't do that, barman—er, I mean, I'd

E 65

rather you didn't. You see, he's had his supper. Just put him to bed.'

There exists an American version, which, very much shorter, ends thus: The bartender says, 'Fine! I'll take it home to dinner.' 'You will *not*,' said the man, handing over the lobster. 'She's had her dinner. Take her to the movies.'

American raconteurs, by the way, delight in telling two other stories about dogs whose exploits take place in raffish surroundings.

A dog goes into a saloon and asks the bartender for a gin, which he drinks without fuss or delay. The dog quietly leaves. The bystanders have been gaping at this civilized performance, and after the dog's departure one of them says to the bartender, 'That's *quite* a dog! Does he always do that?' 'Oh no. He usually drinks whisky.' (A variation has it that the bartender replies, 'Oh no. He usually comes in at seven o'clock.')

The other story concerns a dog and a parrot brought into a bar one day by a regular customer, who, having ordered his drink, says to the dog, 'Now, fella!' And the animal starts a lively conversation with the bird. The performance ends. One of the other customers turns to the owner of these remarkable creatures: 'Say! That's really something.' 'Well, it's not as cute as all that. You

see, the act isn't on the level.' 'No?' 'No. The dog is a ventriloquist.'

B. OTHER QUADRUPEDS

All dogs whatsoever have profited by the favour accorded the shaggy members of the zoological family. Other quadrupeds seem to qualify for admission to the pantheon of 'shaggy dogs'— (1) if they are domesticated and (2) if, like the horse, they are large or, like the mouse, very small, or again, (3) if, like the kangaroo, they are regarded as a national emblem.

Horses fare rather well, as one might expect of creatures almost as intelligent as dogs and so much more presentable. Cats, be it noted, have fared badly, probably because they are so uncannily remote and so intransigently independent and so brashly egocentric: men don't tell friendly little stories about creatures of whom they can only very rarely make friends. Self-sufficiency, like exceptional intelligence, is presumably its own reward; their possessors usually fail to realize how lonely they are. But a good-humoured dog or horse rarely lacks friends.

Of the various 'shaggy dogs' about horses, four call for inclusion in this rigorous selection: the horse that boasted of a Derby win, the horse that played cricket, the horse that ordered martini, and the whisky-drinking horse. Most 'shaggy' horses, you will notice, prefer the rural to the urban air, the field and the meadow to the public-house and the train. Freudians, if any of them survive, will speak glibly of claustrophobia, but perhaps it's merely because horses prefer water to beer.

A townsman was strolling, happy and at his ease, along a bosky lane in the heart of a farming district. The day was perfect, the time his own. Reverie succeeded unto reverie, content to self-congratulation.

His dreaming was interrupted by a cheerful 'Good morning!' He looked to his front, his side, his rear. There was nobody in sight. He thought 'Oh, I must have dreamt it' and was about to resume his stroll when a still more cheerful 'Good morning! *Good* morning!' rendered him most uneasy. He glanced to this side and that, and then up to the fence running along the top of the bank. There he saw a very handsome horse; perhaps, he thought, a racehorse. 'Oh, good morning!' he replied nervously.

'Do you know, I'm a splendid horse?'

'Why, I'm—er—sure you are, old man. Sure you are.'

'You don't *seem* very sure about it. But, my dear sir, I assure you that I really am a splendid, I think I might say a remarkable, horse.'

'Well, if you say so, naturally I believe you.'

'Yes,' continued his new acquaintance, 'I won last year's Derby, you know.'

'Oh, I say! That's magnificent of you.'

'Yes, I suppose it is. Don't think I'll race again. Too exhausting—yes, much too exhausting.'

'But why stop, especially since you're obviously quite exceptional? I mean, it seems a pity and all that.'

The horse went on chatting until they came to the fence debarring him from the next field. 'Well, good day to you, sir. It's been very pleasant chatting to you on this lovely June morning.'

'Good day to *you*, sir.'

A little further along the lane, the townsman

met a farmer, who said, 'Good morning! I suppose my horse has been talking to you?'

'Yes, indeed. Remarkable.'

'Remarkable? I shouldn't say that. By the way, did my horse tell you he had won the Derby?'

'As a matter of fact, I'm afraid he did. But don't be too hard on him. Feeling sociable, I dare say, and saying the first thing that came into his head.'

'A pity! I really must cure him of this shocking habit of telling lies. Too bad of him. Used to be a pretty good horse, you know.'

'Is that so?'

'Yes. Yes, he was. But so untruthful,' as he shook his head slowly and mournfully.

'Ah, well! Don't take the matter too seriously. After all, he may get over it, this bad habit of his.'

'Perhaps, perhaps. But I don't like it. Why, would you believe it, he came only second—yes, a miserable *second*—in that Derby.'

The other horse was, he too, a sportsman; a sportsman in the most truly English of games. His particular story has, admittedly, many variations, but the following version is, I believe, the correct one or, at worst, a trifling variation of the canon.

One of those public-spirited benefactors who do so much to preserve the good health of British national games was taking a cricket team on a short tour of one of the genuinely rural counties. He acted also as captain.

On arriving, early one afternoon, at a village named—well, it might have been named—Mold-on-the-Green, the captain found that one of his team had succumbed to the potency of the cider served at lunch. The fact that this unfortunate man was not the first to have been deceived by that mellow drink did not console their leader for the fact that he was short of a player. He tried to get a substitute from among the villagers, but every available man had been enlisted by the vicar to make a team; the vicar had had his troubles also.

After walking three-quarters of the way round the field, in the vague hope of being able to lure some farm labourer from his labouring, the captain espied a friendly-looking horse, by whose air of exceptional intelligence he felt deeply impressed and in whose hearing he commiserated with himself in these few well-chosen words, 'I'll be the laughing-stock of the village if I have to take the field with one man short.'

'Excuse me, sir,' the horse called to him; 'am I to understand that you have only ten players in all?'

'Yes, indeed. . . . I don't suppose *you*'d care to play, would you?'

'On the contrary, I should be delighted.'

'Good for *you*! Come along with me and I'll open the gate I see just over there.'

The village captain readily agreed to the visitors' team being completed by the inclusion of the horse, 'and', said he magnanimously, 'you may count him as a full member of the team, not merely a substitute.' An hour or so later, the vicar regretted his magnanimity.

The visitors won the toss and went in to bat. At first they did rather badly, six wickets having fallen for a paltry thirty runs. The captain, who had intended to send the horse in as last man, changed his mind: desperate measures were needed; and, well! he wouldn't swear to it, but he thought he saw the horse wink craftily at him. 'Oh, Mr Horse, would you slip on your pads as quickly as you can? I want you to go in.'

'Very good, sir. I have them on.'

'*Have* you? Um—ah, well. Play yourself in. We're rather depending on you, old man.'

'Don't worry, sir. I've been watching these fellows ever since I was a foal. Not what I'd call a really good bowler among the whole lot of 'em.'

For all of one over, that horse played himself

in, cautiously yet efficiently. Then he opened out and scored a century even more speedily than P. G. H. Fender had once done at the Oval. The century scored, he threw away his wicket by getting himself run out. The team made 159 runs in all.

The village team began rather better, yet the visitors dismissed five men with the score at 60; the horse had brilliantly caught three of them, and he continued to field extremely well, never putting a foot wrong, even the villagers applauding his courageous 'stops' and his miraculous anticipations. On one occasion, his captain thought he heard the horse murmuring:

> *And even the ranks of Tuscany*
> *Could scarce forbear to cheer.*

Then the vicar, an ex-Cambridge 'blue', was joined by the village blacksmith, the team's fast bowler and accredited slogger. These two carried the score to 130, to the mighty cheers of the onlookers, enthusiastic supporters every man, woman and child of them.

Worried and even showing that he was worried, the visiting captain went into a huddle with his vice-captain and one or two others. As a result of their agonized deliberation, he beckoned to the horse and said, 'I say, old fellow, we were wondering whether you'd care to bowl. You batted magnificently, your fielding has been superb, probably you're a jolly good bowler too.'

'Are you seriously asking me to bowl?'

'Yes, yes!'

'But that's damn silly, sir! Who has ever heard of a horse *bowling*?'[1]

A neat little story about a horse comes, as one might expect, from America. An unattended horse went into a bar and said to the bartender, 'Gimme a martini.' The bartender complied; the other customers gawked—and swore off liquor. The horse drank the martini, paid for it, said 'Thanks!' and left. The bartender turned calmly to the dazed customers and casually remarked, 'Funny thing. That horse won't drink a martini if it has an olive in it instead of an onion.'

The fourth story may be Australian in origin. The following version is clearly Australian:

An old cocky, who was driving along an outback road in a sulky, pulled into a backblocks pub, stamped across the wooden verandah, and de-

[1] In the United States the same story is told, but more economically, and about a horse that, superb in all other departments of baseball, could not *pitch*.

manded a quart of whisky. 'Put it in a bucket and add a bit of water,' he told the pub-keeper. 'And while you're at it, give me a lady's waist of beer.' The pub-keeper did as he was ordered, but couldn't help remarking: 'That's a helluva small chaser for all that whisky.' The cocky snorted. 'Chaser, be damned,' he said. 'The whisky's for me horse. *I'm* driving.'

After the horse, that other speedy animal, the kangaroo. One or two of the stories about this largest of all the marsupials are rather dull, not to say slow. The following veracious tale, however, has its points.

In a backblocks township of south-western Queensland, the proprietor of the sole public-house was, one swelteringly hot day, serving in the bar. As the regular customers would not be in yet awhile, he was pottering about, doing little odd jobs of cleaning and tidying. He was just a little startled when the door opened and in came a large red kangaroo.

'A small whisky, please!'

'Any particular brand?'

'Oh, any of the stock brands.'

'Very well. That'll be seven shillings and six-pence, mister.'

The kangaroo fumbled in his pouch and drew out three half-crowns and irately planked them down on the counter. He downed his whisky in one capacious swallow and strode towards the door. Bursting with curiosity, the barman exclaimed:

'Excuse me, sir, but this is the first time I've ever served a kangaroo with a whisky. I regard the incident as a good omen.'

Having given the barman a long, cool, level look, in which wonder mingled with contempt, the kangaroo haughtily replied:

"It'll bloody well be the last time too, if you continue to charge seven-and-six for a small whisky.'

Another public-house story, which, however, concerns a London 'pub', is that of a white mouse.[1] Every evening this mouse, ensconced and well concealed in the breast pocket of its owner, would go to the 'local'. The owner always ordered a pint of beer for himself and a tot of whisky; he poured the latter into the breast pocket of his jacket.

Fascinated, the barman let the customer do this two evenings running. But the scarcity of whisky caused him, the next evening, to remonstrate:

[1] In the American version, the mouse is any mouse, colour unspecified.

'Say! what do you mean by wasting that whisky? The stuff is scarce—or haven't you heard?'

An argument ensued. The customer insisted that, so long as he could pay for his drinks, he was entitled to receive them. The barman admitted this, but added the rider, 'Provided you *drink* them.' That, obviously, was dangerous ground. Finally the customer said:

'If you go on talking so daft and so insulting, I'll punch you on the nose.'

'And', squeaked the mouse, peeping indignantly from the whisky-drenched pocket, 'that goes for your cat too.'

Now, that 'shaggy dog' represents the elaboration of a tall story current all over the English-speaking world, at least as early as 1900:

A mouse, living in a wine-cellar, one evening lapped up some cider that the butler had most reprehensibly spilt. An hour later, this mouse was rampaging from one end of the cellar to the other and shouting, 'Where's that damned cat? Put 'em up! Where's that cat? Put 'em up, I said.'

It would be interesting to know how many 'shaggy dogs' have originated in vestigial memories of 'funny stories' or 'tall stories' popular a generation, perhaps two generations earlier. The following American story, however, is pure 'shaggy dog':

One day a man came into a saloon and produced a mouse from his pocket and set it down on the bar in front of him. When the ordered drink arrived—the bartender and the other customers were meanwhile in a virtual coma—the mouse, standing on tiptoe, sipped it and then, in a fine bass voice, sang 'Annie Laurie'. The neighbouring customer asked the mouse's owner to sell him. 'Hell!' said the owner. 'Buy me a drink and I'll *give* him to you.' The amazed and gratified neighbouring customer bought the drink, pocketed the mouse, and departed rejoicing. 'You must be nuts, man,' expostulated the bartender, 'why did you give a gold mine like *that* away?' 'Hell!' replied the ex-owner, 'the only song that mouse *can* sing is "Annie Laurie".'

The next drama concerns another mouse, with a rat playing 'second lead':

Dissatisfied with his lodgings ('Too many cats and dogs, too few pickings'), a rat went looking for more suitable quarters. He soon found a house that seemed to be a considerable improvement. Going into the dining-room, he saw a mouse running gaily about on the sideboard.

'Hullo, there! What sort of lodgings are these?'

'Fine,' answered the mouse.

'Any cats?'

'None at all.'

'But there are dogs, I suppose?'

'No dogs either.'

'What's the food like?'

'Fine.'

So off the rat went to the larder. He had only just started on a most appetizing wedge of cheese when a huge tomcat leaped on him. Making a desperate effort, the rat managed to escape, but not without leaving half his tail behind. He was about to return to the dining-room, in order to ask his little friend the meaning of this unfortunate incident and was, in fact, walking along a passage, when from an open door a large, very fierce dog rushed at him. In the ensuing fight, the rat, who was no mean 'scrapper', lost an ear and a great deal of fur.

More indignant than shaken, the rat reconnoitred the space still to be traversed, made sure that the way was clear, and slipped into the dining-room, where the mouse, who seemed to be in high spirits, was still cavorting on the sideboard.

'Look, you miserable little pipsqueak, what the

hell do you mean by telling me that this is a house fit for any rat to live in? I'm lucky to be still alive. First a ruddy great cat and then a very ill-tempered dog!'

'Oh,' the mouse replied happily, 'you mustn't take any notice of *me*, I've been drinking hard since eight o'clock this morning.'

The next two stories are indigenous to Australia. They are told here as my friend Sidney J. Baker has told them to me.

An anteater was ambling along the bank of a

F

creek when he happened to look in the water and saw his reflection. 'Hallo,' he thought. 'Another anteater, I guess. Cooling off. Pretty sensible in this weather.' Since they had not been introduced, he nodded pleasantly, and the reflection nodded in return, and he continued his journey. Later that day he was returning near the same spot and looked in the creek again. The reflection was still there. He nodded again and, seeing the reflection nod also, was moved to speak. 'I hesitate to interfere in what is obviously a private matter,' he observed, 'but you're a bit of a mug sticking round here. The ants which our species finds necessary for survival are on higher ground.'

'Ar, nuts!' the other replied. 'I prefer fish.'

A bandicoot, a wombat and a goanna decided to hold a party. They threw in for a couple of gallons of steam, a keg of beer and a packet of sandwiches each, and settled down to drink themselves silly. A couple of days later, in one of their lucid moments, they reassessed their stock and found that it had dwindled somewhat. 'Someone'll have to go for a bit more bombo,' said the bandicoot, 'but it looks as though the sandwiches will last us out.' So they drew lots to see who should

go, and the lot fell to the goanna. After putting
on an act and mumbling to himself about the
unfairness of fortune, the goanna took up the
money and went out. An hour passed, then two,
and still he had not returned. At nightfall the
bandicoot and the wombat were still waiting.
'Looks as though the so-and-so has shot through

on us,' said the wombat. The bandicoot was in-
clined to agree. 'Maybe he'll be back in the morning,' he said hopefully. Next morning, the goanna
had still not returned, and the friends were bitter
in their denunciation of him. They coupled his
name with the most forceful adjectives. Just at the
moment that their vituperation reached its peak,
the goanna put his head in the door. 'If you chaps
don't turn it up,' he said sharply, 'I won't go at
all.'

The 'Shaggy Dog' Itself

Many years ago *Collier's Weekly* published, implicatively as reminiscence, a 'shaggy dog' that must, by any criterion, rank very high.

On a hot summer afternoon a couple of hippopotamuses were basking in the turbid waters of the Nile with their nostrils showing just above the surface. They appeared to be very contented and even a little drowsy. Finally one of them raised his snout and said dreamily, 'Somehow, you know, I can't help thinking that this is Thursday.'

C. FISH

'Shaggy dogs' concerning fish do not often occur. The following, however, is of good quality.

A man in a hurry went into a smart West End restaurant. A waiter hurried to his table. 'Haven't time for a proper meal. Just bring me a sardine on toast and a lager.' The dish appeared. The diner was about to stick his fork into the sardine, when, to his amazement, the fish said, 'Please don't eat me. I had a very bad time in the Bay of Biscay; the wife is ill; and the young 'uns haven't eaten a square meal for days.' Taking pity on the unfortunate sardine, the man called the waiter over and said, 'Look! I find that I can't even stay to eat. Bring me the bill, please.' The tactful waiter said nothing, although he did rather wonder.

A couple of hours later, the man, now outrageously hungry, went into a respectable restaurant and ordered a sardine on toast. The dish was served. The man was just about to impale the sardine, when, to his still greater amazement, the sardine said, 'Please don't eat me. Oh, it's *you*, sir. Well, my story is true. Things are really very bad. You can see that I've been thrown out of that West End place.' The man thought it all very odd: but he spared the fish and ate only the toast.

Perhaps a fortnight later, the same man went into a rather scruffy little restaurant in Soho, the hour being much too late for him to obtain a meal elsewhere. He ordered a sardine on toast—a dish that, as you will have gathered, he liked inordinately. The dish arrived. Before he had more than glanced at it, the sardine said, 'Fancy meeting you in *Soho*, of all places!'

D. INSECTS

The following story is of interest, for a reason that will appear:

From reading about the performing fleas of Paris, a certain idle fellow suddenly formed the idea that he would like to have something of the sort. He diligently collected half a dozen fleas and enthusiastically trained them to jump. Soon they excelled at both the high and the long jump, taken either individually or as a team leaping abreast. He had only to say 'Jump!' and they jumped: but he never knew whether they would jump high or broad; nor, apparently, did they. After many attempts to train them to high-jump when he called 'High!', and to broad-jump when he called 'Broad!', he wearied of such unrewarding labour.

Then he had a bright idea. He cut off their legs. He knew that they wouldn't be able to jump very far, but he was nonplussed when, after repeatedly bidding them jump, he finally had to admit that they no longer could. Being of a thoughtful, studious frame of mind, he sat down, in the most comfortable chair, in order to think it out.

After an hour's concentrated thought, he went to the kitchen, where his wife was preparing the evening meal. 'Do you know, Mary,' he said, 'I've just made a most notable entomological discovery. Fleas,' he concluded portentously, 'have their brains in their legs.'

That story presents a *non sequitur* of logic, and not, as in the overwhelming majority of 'shaggy dog' stories, a *non sequitur* of psychology. The sudden unexpectedness that characterizes the conclusion of every 'shaggy dog' contains, it is manifest, a *non sequitur*, not of faulty logic, but of attitude and response.

The fleas story, although it resembles a 'shaggy dog', strictly isn't one. It stands on a par with this other example of humorously faulty reasoning, an example I quote in order to emphasize the duty laid solemnly upon all of us—to avoid the temptation of supposing that an alluring *non sequitur* is necessarily a 'shaggy dog'.

The example, however:

An undergraduate, who was taking an Honours course in Philosophy, met a friend—a visitor and a much older man. This friend told him that he could hardly call himself a philosopher until he learned much more of the world or, at any rate, became more of a man of the world; rightly or wrongly, he tried to educate him in wines and spirits. The young fellow disliked wine, so he concentrated on spirits.

One evening he drank nothing but whisky and soda. The next morning he woke with a very sore head. Two evenings later he switched to brandy and soda; the next morning, he woke with a head no less sore. After a suitable interval he passed an evening in the company of rum and soda; as a result of this foul combination, which only a Stoic philosopher could have brought himself to drink, he had, next morning, an even worse headache.

'This won't do at all,' he said, communing with his better self. 'Obviously something is wrong somewhere. It couldn't have been the whisky, for I drank only the best whisky. It couldn't have been the brandy, for that too was a very superior brand. Nor yet the rum, which, as everyone, knows is medicinal. *Ergo*, it must have been the soda.'

From that day to this, he has never touched soda.

E. BIRDS

There is a paucity of good 'shaggy dogs' about birds, I don't quite know why. The following love-story, however, is rather charming.

In Trafalgar Square lived a boy pigeon; at Saint Paul's a girl pigeon. One day as they were expressing the exuberance of youth by flying over the London they had already adopted as their district, they almost flew into each other over the Law Courts. They looked. They fell in love.

They courted very happily. They met every day,

alternately on the dome of Saint Paul's and on Nelson's Column.

One glorious morning in early May, when hearts as well as birds were singing, the rendezvous was for eleven o'clock in Trafalgar Square. Usually so prompt, the girl pigeon had not arrived by 11.5 and the boy pigeon was beginning to feel anxious. At 11.15 he was pacing along a balustrade; before that, he had flown over the Square, first this way, then that; such was his agony of spirit that the poor fellow hardly knew what he was doing.

Just when he was about to ring Whitehall 1212 and ask the police whether any serious accident had been reported—by now, it must have been all of 11.20—he saw his little friend strolling gaily down the steps of the National Gallery. For a moment he felt quite faint with relief. Having pulled himself together, he hastened to meet her. He was on the point of telling her of the distress she had caused him, when she said:

'Darling, I'm *so* sorry. Do forgive me, Georgie dear. But it was such a lovely morning I thought I'd *walk*.'[1]

[1] This conclusion occurs in an Australian story about a mopoke that, invited to a dinner, excuses himself to his host with 'It was such a lovely evening'. The way these 'shaggy dogs' get around!

F. HUMAN BEINGS

In the following stories we do not see men at either their spiritual or their intellectual best. We do see them in a whimsical and occasionally endearing light. This, after all, is not a *magnum opus* devoted to research into man's moral and immoral nature, but merely a monograph; exploratory, not exhaustive, of one small aspect of his creative genius.

A certain quite harmless and, to give him his due, most worthy fellow went to live in a district new to him. Following his antique habit, he sought a public-house congenial to his temperament and considerate of his purse, and, born lucky, he found one, only five minutes' walk from the house that, in twenty years' time, he would perhaps own.

Whether it was that the air of his new habitat over-exhilarated him or that the beer contained an illogically greater content of alcohol than that to which he had latterly been accustomed, he started a most extraordinary habit. He would slowly drink his pint and then walk up the wall on the near side of the room, topsy-turvily step smartly along the ceiling and then, with immense

dignity, down the opposite wall. This acrobatic feat exercised a cathartic influence: radiant of face, yet saying not a single word, he would put on his hat, walk firmly and impeccably to the door, and then, like the good citizen he was, go straight home.

One evening a stranger witnessed this somewhat odd performance. The performer gone, the stranger turned to the barman and asked:

'Does that fellow often come in here?'

'Yes, every night.'

'And does he always act in that extraordinary manner?'

'Oh, yes! But, bless you, sir, we don't take any notice: he *never* says "Goodnight".'

Whereas that story, I suspect, arose from some raconteur's probably subconscious desire to record his lively appreciation of the average Englishman's imperturbability, the following absurdity perhaps satirizes the tendency of mankind to ignore the comfortable profundity of the pragmatic adage, 'Don't worry! It may never happen.' From the almost too numerous variants, I select this:

A middle-aged man and his wife went to the theatre, where, contrary to their expectation of seeing a bright English comedy, replete with good, clean fun and plenty of heartily obvious jokes, they sat through a bitter-sweet, disillusioned, highly sophisticated French comedy. The man felt, as men usually do, more depressed than his wife, who never took such things to heart.

After the performance, they decided to hail a taxi. Not unnaturally, they had to wait some time. A man standing near them succeeded in capturing a taxi, and, turning to the married pair, said:

'You take it. I think I'll walk. But before I go, would you please give me a light—I've left my lighter at home and don't carry matches.'

'I'm awfully sorry. 'Fraid I haven't, either.'

'Ah well, can't be helped. Good night!'

'Good night—and thank you for the taxi.'

'Think nothing of it. *Good* night!'

No sooner had they seated themselves comfortably in the taxi they were so very lucky to be occupying, the woman exclaimed:

'That was rather mean of you, John. You know you have both lighter and matches.'

'Well, you never know how these things will end.'

'Why, John, what on earth *do* you mean?'

'Oh, I know, Mary, it sounds rather silly. But I felt that, if I gave him a light, there'd be no knowing where it'd stop. Don't you see? First of all, I give him a light. We start chatting. He seems a very nice fellow, so I offer him a lift in the taxi he so kindly got hold of for us. When we arrive at the house, I'm bound to invite him to come in for a drink. We talk some more and find that we like each other; that he likes you, and you him. Then he invites me to dine at his club. I don't belong to one, so, as I can't afford to dine him at an expensive restaurant, we have him here for dinner.

'And that's when the real trouble begins. Kathie has just left school and is at a most impressionable age. She falls in love with him and, because she's an attractive—a *very* attractive—girl, he falls too. Being old-fashioned, he asks for my blessing.

'Now, my dear, how can I possibly approve of a match between my darling Kathie and this man —this man who doesn't even possess one?'

(Which rather goes to show that some middle-aged men are old women.)

During the latter half of 1951 there was a Holy Year story going the rounds; it still does. I myself did not hear it until mid-October 1952. Like many other 'shaggy dogs', although it can be told as a fairly short story it is usually rather long: and that rare creature the natural storyteller will, if he be in the mood, spin it out until it attains the dimensions of a full-dress short story. For me, it loses its flavour by being concise and its savour by being diffuse. I tell it, therefore, in what I conceive to be a mean; to some, inevitably, that will not be a golden mean. One cannot please everyone. But then, he who tries to please everyone succeeds only in pleasing no one, least of all himself.

PADDY'S VISIT TO ROME

Early in Holy Year, Paddy went to see the parish priest on some business or other. (It doesn't matter what it was.) The business over, the priest said to Paddy:

'Paddy, as you know, this is Holy Year and all those who can are making the journey to Rome. Your farm, though small, is prospering. It won't be easy, perhaps, for you to get away, but if you choose a fairly slack time of the year, your good wife Biddy will manage it very capably for you. So what about it?'

'Well, Father, I suppose I could. Tell you what: if Biddy says "Yes", I'll go.'

'I hoped you'd say that. You *ought* to go, if you can.'

'Very well, Father, I'll see what Biddy has to say.'

So Paddy returned home and called his wife. 'Biddy, the Father was saying, Why don't I go to Rome, seeing it's Holy Year and all. Do you think you could run the place if I go in time to get back home a little before harvest-time?'

'Why, Paddy, I'm thinking it's a fine idea. And you can tell me all about it. Och, it's proud and glad I am that you should be going to Rome to see the Holy Father. You'll be the only man in the village to be making that fine journey.'

Biddy decided that her Patrick should do it in style. He would—from Dublin, at least—travel all the way by air.

At the Irish airport, Paddy was surprised and delighted when, a few minutes before the 'plane was due to take off, a very important dignitary of the Church arrived in a car and, hastening over to him, said:

'Paddy, we're delighted that you should be going to Rome and representing your village there. We want you to convey Eire's respects and loyalty to the Holy Father, and I myself should be most grateful if you gave him my personal good wishes—very respectfully, Paddy.'

Paddy said that he would gladly do this. Full

of pride and joyous wonderment, he boarded the 'plane. Nor did his pride and happiness suffer abatement when, at the London airport, an even more exalted personage told him how delighted he was that Paddy should be making the pilgrimage and added that he would be grateful if *his* country's and his own private greetings and assurances of loyalty were conveyed to His Holiness. This, Paddy promised to do.

Arriving at the airport outside Rome, Paddy was about to enter the bus chartered to take pilgrims to their lodgings in the Eternal City, when an alert young priest hurried over to him and exclaimed:

'No, Paddy, there is a car waiting for you; and in it is Cardinal ——, who wishes to speak to you. Of course, you know all about the Cardinal?'

Paddy didn't, but he had no intention of displaying his ignorance. 'Of *course*,' he said, 'a lovely man.' The priest beamed. Paddy was conducted to the very fine car. The presentation over, the Cardinal said:

'Paddy, we all want you to know that we're delighted, and much affected, by your coming all that long way from your little village'—Paddy didn't altogether like that, for he thought Bally-something-or-other a considerable place, but he wisely kept silent—'to pay your respects and perform your devotions in the home of the Holy Church. We are proud of you.'

With a natural dignity and no embarrassment whatever, Paddy thanked the Cardinal for his handsome words.

'Now, Paddy,' the Cardinal said, 'I am taking you straight to his Holiness the Pope.'

Without a moment's delay, Paddy was conducted into the presence. The Pope received him very graciously and spoke at some length to this loyal son. Paddy, who knew his place, was beginning to say farewell, but his Holiness stopped him.

'Don't go just yet, Paddy. I must go out on the balcony and bless the crowd. I should like you to come out with me. You have only to stand at my side—though a little behind me; you won't speak. No need to be shy, man. It'll soon be over.'

Embarrassed at last, yet very happy, Paddy followed his Holiness on to the balcony.

Among those watching the ceremony were the Soviet envoy and his personal assistant.

'Tell me, Ivan,' said the envoy, nudging his assistant, who was regarding the scene with a definitely non-atheistic air, '*who* is that, standing there with Paddy?'

The 'Shaggy Dog' Itself

That story was told me by a Catholic, in an inimitable Irish brogue. The humour of it, however, depends, not on a brogue nor on an ability to speak Anglo-Irish: but simply on the essential 'shagginess' and the delicious *non sequitur*. The next story is very different in its characters and its setting and might easily have been turned by A. J. Alan into one of his unparallelled tales, with an element of suspense and mystery.

The Hole

In an outer suburb of London—or, as it might be, Liverpool or Birmingham or Glasgow or Belfast—two friends had adjoining houses. The wives became friends. They were, in short, all friends together.

They were also rivals, the Smiths and the Robinsons. Oh! in the nicest, most harmless way. They were gardeners, keen and industrious and well-informed. If the Smiths succeeded with roses, the Robinsons promptly ascertained whether they could do the same; naturally, they did. If the Robinsons proved that with the most niggling and delicate plants they had the greenest of green thumbs, the Smiths immediately showed that their thumbs were no less green.

This happy and prosperous rivalry extended to what is quaintly known as 'garden furniture'. Chairs rivalled chairs, rural bench vied with rural bench; gnomes and elves, rabbits and squirrels, urns and sundials, strove in stone to attain an improbable supremacy.

And then, one glowing day, Mrs Smith had a 'marvellous' idea. At the week-end, she and her husband dug a very large hole in the middle of

the front lawn. The Robinsons waited to see what their neighbours were going to do with this hole. 'Lily pond, do you think? or perhaps a tiny sunken garden?' But the Smiths did nothing with the hole, except to prevent it from silting up. The Robinsons, after several agonizing weeks, decided that this hole must represent something emblematic 'or do we mean symbolic?'

There was nothing for it, the Robinsons thought, but to have, in their front lawn, a hole that should resemble, as nearly as possible, that in the Smiths' lawn. But Mr and Mrs Robinson shared an aversion to digging as strenuous as this. So they, or rather Mrs Robinson, wrote to a well-known firm of landscape gardeners and ordered a hole, so many feet in diameter and so many in depth.

Two days later, she received a letter:

DEAR MADAM,

We regret to say that, at the moment, we have not in stock a hole of the dimensions you require. But, if you wish us to do so, we will advise you when one becomes available.

Yours faithfully,

———

The Robinsons waited, not very patiently.

Sooner than they had expected, they received a second letter:

DEAR MADAM,

We count ourselves fortunate in being able to offer you, not exactly what you required but something we hope will serve equally well and perhaps better: a hole one foot deeper and eighteen inches more in diameter. The client who had ordered it has had to cancel his order, for he is emigrating to Kenya and selling his house.

To accommodate you, we are prepared to charge for this larger hole the same price we should have charged for one of the size you specified.

Awaiting your esteemed instructions,

Yours faithfully,

⸻

The Robinsons were so excited that they wired their acceptance. The same day, the reply came: 'Delivery to-morrow afternoon.'

The hole was being transported in a huge truck, driven by Alf, accompanied by Bert, who would keep his eye on the valuable load. They took their work very seriously, these two, and Alf constantly asked Bert whether the hole was safe. For instance, when they approached a railway bridge, 'Height twelve feet', they anxiously debated whether the clearance was sufficient. Bert, having measured the total height of truck and load, said 'Six inches to spare', and Alf replied, 'I'll have to drive very smoothly, or I'll knock the head off that blinking hole.'

He did, and all was well. All continued to go well until, only two and a quarter miles from their destination, they came to a very steep hill.

'Watch it, Bert. We don't want the thing slipping from its moorings.'

'All right.'

Just before they reached the crest and while, in fact, they were congratulating each other on having 'done it', they heard a very odd noise, as of something plopping on to the road behind them.

'Strike a light, Alf, that [unmentionable] hole has fallen off. You'll have to pull up at the top, and I'll go and see what's the matter.'

'Cor! What a thing to happen, Bert? The boss won't half be wild if we've lost that [equally unmentionable] hole.'

At the top of the rise, Alf pulled up. Bert hastily descended and ran back to where they had heard that queer plopping noise.

Bert did not return. Alf became anxious and then more and more alarmed. Finally he walked back to find out what had happened; but his pal was never seen again.

Bert had fallen down the hole.

*   *   *

Such is the 'shaggy dog': a story that, usually told in a leisurely manner (as inaugurated by A. J. Alan), is inconsequent and, in some instances, absurd. The final touch—a sudden and unexpected conclusion—contains a striking *non sequitur* that, in the purest form of the genre, is psychological, the merely logical *non sequitur* being rare. In addition to being either humorous or witty or, indeed, both, the 'shaggy dog' is, with very rare exceptions, notably clean. Moreover, it shows a warm appreciation and a deep understanding, not only of human nature but also of quadrupeds and of even humbler forms of life. It is, I think, this warm humanity which accounts for the popularity and the long life of this rather odd, yet unaffected and unpretentious form of literary art.

Index

Index

Index